Breaking

Grand Silence

Breaking

A Former Catholic Priest Speaks Out

Grand Silence

Marvin Josaitis, PhD

TATE PUBLISHING
AND ENTERPRISES, LLC

Published by Tate Publishing & Enterprises, LLC
127 E. Trade Center Terrace | Mustang, Oklahoma 73064 USA
1.888.361.9473 | www.tatepublishing.com

Tate Publishing is committed to excellence in the publishing industry. The company reflects the philosophy established by the founders, based on Psalm 68:11,
"The Lord gave the word and great was the company of those who published it."

Book design copyright © 2011 by Tate Publishing, LLC. All rights reserved.
Cover design by Joel Uber
Interior design by Sarah Kirchen

Published in the United States of America

ISBN: 978-1-61346-678-0
1. Biography & Autobiography / Personal Memoirs
2. Biography & Autobiography / Religious
11.09.20

Dedication

I wrote the book when the Catholic Church's pains of pedophilia emerged. My tale, hopefully, offers insights into not only the sexual aberrations associated with the current reality but also the universal realities surrounding maturation, freedom, and identification with "every man's" struggle for meaning and purpose.

Hence, I dedicate this book to the victims, known and unknown, who have suffered at the hands as well as the teachings of aberrant religious and pedophiliac clergy who in their own inadequate humanity have chosen to sexually, emotionally, and psychologically violate the precious trust given to them. In the name of God, these innocent and trusting faithful have been robbed of the total richness and beauty of life which otherwise could have been.

Acknowledgments

There are so many philosophers, theologians, and novelists whom I wish to acknowledge, but especially S. Kierkegaard and the many existentialists (atheistic and Christian) who followed him—most notably, Gabriel Marcel. All of these brilliant writers, too numerous to mention, shaped and lead me out of a traditional and static scholastic philosophy espoused by the Catholic Church, a philosophy so remote from my life and my life experiences. Thomas S. Kuhn's *The Structure of Scientific Revolutions* merits special commendation with my deepest appreciation.

No one can understand this book without understanding the contributions to my life—both indirect and direct—from all my family, but especially Frank W. and Margaret A. Josaitis (my parents), Edwidge Sauvé Girard (my maternal grandmother), the three grandparents I never was privileged to know and touch (Noé Girard, Franz and Ursula Zalenka Josaitis), Norman (my only sibling), and the woman with whom I have shared over forty years of beautiful marriage: Donna Marie Rimer. In acknowledging them, I will share pertinent features of these relationships to help the reader comprehend the full meaning of this book.

Finally, I wish to acknowledge two Detroit heroes of mine—simple men who have embodied the spirit of the gospel message throughout their fourscore years: Thomas Kerwin, a former priest who is now married and lives with his equally remarkable wife, Betty, in Colorado Springs; and Thomas J. Gumbleton, retired bishop of the Catholic Archdiocese of Detroit, who remains a stellar example of what bishops should be. Both men live their distinctive caring and giving lives as powerful statements to Christians who hopefully will journey back to the radical truth their churches espouse, but which I rarely see exhibited in its fullness.

Table of Contents

Prologue

"The unexamined life is not worth living." Socrates

Not even Socrates could have prepared me for the shocking sexual events that occurred hours before I was ordained a Catholic priest. I had prepared for twelve years in three seminaries for this sacred moment. But I had not even the faintest clue that a friend would—could—be sexually violated in our seminary residence quarters hours before we both processed into the cathedral as deacons and exited as priests. And more, violated by a most unexpected and uninvited intruder! What had happened physically and emotionally to him caused deep anguish for me.

Naively, I had assumed that an examined life has some analytical time parameters. Quite the contrary: now I would need to re-examine my life as a priest with new, albeit unwanted, information to see if my newly accepted life as a priest was indeed worth living. Fortified with sound logic and intellectual honesty, I continued examining my life. I observed other priests and religious carefully under different microscopes. But more, I continued to understand and uncover the basic erroneous paradigms underlying Church teaching on—and its basic mistrust of—sexuality.

Within two years, I started anew. I had no choice if I were to remain faithful to myself and have, indeed, a life worth living. I resigned the priesthood and moved onto Robert Frost's road less traveled, "and that has made all the difference."

Immigrant Beginnings: Eastern Europe

No one would remember. Like so many immigrants to the United States at the turn of the twentieth century, their lives would be lost in time. Unless... unless someone realized a century later that Franz Yesaides and his wife, Ursula Zalenka, a young married couple in their early twenties, decided to put their feet to their dreams: a better life for themselves, their young daughter, and the future children they hoped to raise. With little material wealth and little formal education but confidence in themselves and bolstered by a strong religious faith, Franz and Ursula began their journey from Lithuania, never looking back. They sojourned in Germany, picking up the odd jobs that Franz's practical technical skills and fierce work ethic permitted, saving what they could in order to continue their journey eventually to the new world—America.

While in Germany, their second child was born. Pregnant with their third, they finally could afford the voyage "economy class á la 1907" to Ellis Island where the intake officer wrote their names as "Frank and Ursula Josaitis." They had been renamed and baptized as Americans. The few cousins who had preceded them lived in Detroit, soon to be the new home for their daughter and two sons.

Reaching Detroit in time to be part of Henry Ford's auto revolution, my grandfather, Frank, worked in maintenance at the Rouge plant for the now famous $5.00 per day. Their fourth child and third son, my father, was born February 16, 1909. Their family was completed with a birth of another daughter prior to the start of World War I.

My father, Frank, left school at age sixteen to help my grandfather support not only his sister but an ill invalid mother. His older siblings were adults out of the nest, living the typical lives of first generation immigrants of the time, forging new lives in a new country, trying not to give signs of the Old World. My father, however, never forgot his roots and wasn't ashamed of parents who reflected another culture.

I wish that I had known my grandparents. Both died, however, during the 1930s, and I was born on December 27, 1941, twenty days after Pearl Harbor. Whenever I visit Detroit, I try to drive by the house on the hill above Fort Street where they lived. Now, perhaps, it isn't there anymore except in my memory. My grandparents lived hard lives but fulfilled their dreams long before they reached their middle years. But each died at relatively young ages three decades after arriving in Detroit, with other dreams yet unfulfilled. They left their children and eventually their grandchildren whom they never watched grow up, and consequently they never experienced themselves the heritage of an America where all could be possible for them and their family. Their tough immigrant lives were to be fulfilled by their offspring.

Franz and Ursula's perseverance, their work ethic, their trust in themselves, their willingness to make their dreams a reality, their drive and spirit, their satisfaction with delayed gratification, their commitment to family, and their desire to make the future their present happiness have influenced my values and life dramatically. Strange how two people who are only known through a faded photograph and a few overheard reminiscences from family gatherings can have such a profound effect on a boy growing up. No one would remember. But through at least me and hopefully through their great grandchildren who will only know them through these pages of time, their lives will continue to be relived anew.

Immigrant Beginnings: French Canada

Edwidge Sauvé was a tough but soft woman—a peasant, a woman of the fields with less than eight (and possibly only four) years of formal education. She farmed with her family in a French community of southwestern Ontario until she met Noé Girard, who was several years her senior. Edwidge was a teenager when she married and continued to farm, now with Noé. They had ten children in Canada, one of whom died falling out of a walnut tree during their first twelve years of marriage. As is the custom within most French Canadian families, grandparents frequently are referred to as "Pipi" and "Mimi," warm, colloquial names easy for children to say at an early age. So it was in our family.

In 1912, Pipi (age fifty-four) and Mimi (age forty-six) piled their remaining nine children and whatever belongings they could fit into a horse-drawn wagon crossing the Detroit River on a barge into Michigan. Theirs was another immigrant tale of the early twentieth century. When they arrived "states-side" to fulfill their dream of a better life for their children, I suspect that they had a few dollars with them—but maybe only pennies.

Marguerite (later changed to Margaret), their last child, was born in the USA on February 28, 1915. Edwidge was forty-nine and Noé fifty-seven. Noé died two years later from a serious asthma condition, supporting his large family as a night watchman in the Ternstedt GM motor plant in Detroit. Another older son died shortly after that as a young man in a tragic train-track accident. And so his middle-aged farm-girl widow without a farm did what she knew best—she cleaned homes part-time in a wealthy suburb of Detroit and cleaned rooms as well as cooked for the veterans housed at Fort Wayne. After her eldest four were married, three teenage children left school after the eighth grade to help her earn enough money to raise their two youngest siblings, ages two and eleven. A teenage niece and nephew, whom she also raised, helped with the family coffer as well. She insisted eventually that her youngest child would be the first to finish high school. As her youngest, Margaret was going to be raised like all other American girls and wouldn't have to worry about cleaning other peoples' homes for a living.

A year after she graduated from high school, Margaret married Frank Josaitis. Edwidge was invited to live with the newly married couple for the next fourteen years, until her death at age eighty-two in 1948. She helped raise two more boys—my brother, Norman, and me.

I have lived through the life and death of only one grandparent, my Mimi, Edwidge Sauvé Girard. I was the baby of her baby. She was the only grandparent that I knew. During her life our home buzzed with people. Someone would come to visit—an elderly relative from Canada, an occasional grand-uncle or aunt, someone related whom she had raised. She was the matriarch of the family. She was love incarnate to me and to the myriad of distant relatives who would come to visit, be they great-uncles, great-aunts, or distant cousins. Her life centered around her nine living children, their spouses, and her more than thirty grandchildren and great-grandchildren. And I was privileged to be the last of her clan!

I was nearly seven when I attended my first wake. I remember touching Mimi's cold hand but was reassured that God had called her to a better place where she could be happy again. No one had much of an answer for me when I asked, "Why was it then that everyone is crying if Mimi was happy now?" Somehow I didn't comprehend that life would be different without my Mimi. And I wasn't able to comprehend until much later in life how difficult the years after were for my mother who had lived for thirty-three years with her mother always under the same roof in one dependent form or another. I couldn't comprehend how my dad must have felt losing the second mother he loved so much. And I was incapable of realizing that my brother who would have been her baby grandson for nearly seven years before my arrival on the scene had now lost a significant part of his life as a young teenager.

Even though I was nearly seven years old, with my Mimi went a lifetime of my memories to which nothing could ever be added. My life stopped with her for that instant, and that early winter day that she died, I cast in stone a part of me that had died as well. She was singular in my life and in the lives of my family—a special treasure, never to be replaced. I have romanticized a small youth's infatuation with a woman larger than life, but she holds a special part of her youngest grandchild's heart to this day, and always will. She was the singular contact with my ancestry whom I could touch and love. At day's end, she was my memory of a childhood long gone, yet a relationship that I will always cling to regardless of its accuracy. We were special to each other; we shared a short moment in time that lives on as though her lullabies to me have played on forever.

My youth was immensely influenced by relationships. Throughout life I have often discovered that the baby of the family absorbs the memories of the family members, listening as each retells the events. Often I can't separate what are my own memories from those of my relatives. The prolific author, Joyce Carol Oates, wrote with the persistence and faith and hope in the ultimate values inherent in family life: "You never give such relationships a thought living them. To give a thought—to take thought—is a function of dissociation, distance. You can't exercise memory until you've removed yourself from memory's source."[1]

Through Mimi, I ultimately realized that families are made by working on it; it is an active and constant creation from whomever is involved. And, ultimately, we grow as individuals in finding out who we really are, what we believe, and what we stand for. Families don't just happen. Families are made.

A Charmed Life

Growing up with Frank and Margaret Josaitis was a gift that neither my brother, Norman, nor I had done anything to deserve. The love and attention that they showered on us daily was only surpassed by the love and attention they continually demonstrated for each other. The two of them had given themselves to each other on July 3, 1934, and their love vows lasted a lifetime together—nearly fifty years. They were really a romantic couple in an unassuming, quiet way, much like the characters in Virginia Woolf's deservedly acclaimed *To the Lighthouse*. Whether expressed in words or not, to live under the same roof with my mom and dad was to know that a stream-of-consciousness love affair was constantly in the making.

During my upper high school years, my fascination with Virginia Woolf's novels mysteriously brought me back to the Frank and Margaret I watched carefully as my models and heroes in life. Moments would emerge when they would simply be looking at each other or sitting in the same room, and their countenance quietly shouted, "We live a wonderful life together." Disagreements and voiced anger were rare, but when they emerged, the salve of love endured. What eventually transpired brought anew a beautiful sunrise or sunset to move on beyond the insignificance of the moment, given the exigencies of the lifetime ahead. Norman and I realize today that we hadn't deserved their wonderful gifts of simple and genuine humanity carved into the beautiful, unassuming parents that they were.

Maybe the times also helped. The 1940s, with the war, the rationing, the concern for one's fellow man whether here or abroad, the simplified lifestyles—all of these, perhaps, helped to focus on what is really important in life. And the post-war years of the early '50s continued the movement for national recovery, with everyone chipping in. I guess, at the end, that our more complex, highly technological fast-paced lifestyle today clouds the value of the times to which I refer.

During our formative dependent years of life, my parents spent time with their two sons. We listened to the radio shows together and laughed together and discussed what was being said together. We went to movies together. We prepared food together. We were a unit whose very existence depended upon constant attention to one another's well-being.

I never remember being with a hired babysitter. After my Mimi died, whenever my parents visited friends or relatives, my brother and I went with them. If we got tired, we simply crawled up on a nearby couch and waited for the welcoming call, "It's time to go home." And their friends or relatives became part of the village family that was raising us to be the future men, the standard-bearers for society. Consequently, we were included in everything "real" transpiring around us: the problems occurring in lives around us, the events in other people's lives, the good and the bad, the joys and the sorrows, and—ultimately—death. Nothing was kept from us. We were expected to be part of and involved in life's joys and life's vicissitudes. This was Gail Sheehy's *Passages* being experienced and lived at every turn. Mom and Dad did not shelter us from reality. And they didn't shelter us from their interpretations of what growing up and living meant.

Had I not known better, I would conclude today that they had been schooled in C.S. Lewis' *Mere Christianity*. Their religious faith was more a true spirituality not drenched in guilt, dogma, prescriptive judgmentalism; they indeed respected people who were different. In addition to going to church together, we had our daily and weekly rituals around the home.

Going to school was our workday. No excuses, no absences unless through sickness, and keeping noses to the grindstone. Our parents supported and reinforced the teachers, even if we complained or moaned; they knew the value of maintaining discipline and authority inside and outside the home. We quickly learned that, had we acted inappropriately during the school day, we would be heard—but Mom and Dad would never create a conflict with due authority. They would express openly their concern about our feelings but would also express their disappointment that we had not acted appropriately to those who carried on their responsibility as parents under a different role: teacher. Disappointing behavior with teachers reflected back as disappointing behavior with parents. And so Mom and Dad reinforced responsible authority in our lives.

Thinking back fifty-sixty years, our family life combined play and work. Norman and I had assignments that justified an allowance, which we could use to purchase the "non-essentials." Our parents were meticulous do-it-your-selfers and taught us the proper way of maintaining a lawn, landscaping, and gardening. Inside the home, we learned how to paint, wallpaper, repair, and use tools. Projects were accomplished together. Our home formed a microcosm of life: work, play, shelter, support, and love.

We were given the desire to advance in education to the highest level we could. Our father instilled that we could become anything in life with hard work and perseverance, with one exception: we couldn't become meat-cutters. That was his job, and he made it a point to not teach us his skills. He expected different directions from his sons. We were given the desire to help others, especially those less fortunate in life. The parish priests and teachers were often held up as examples of that.

Our parents were preeminent examples of strong work ethics, honesty, and fidelity. Their mottos were simplistic truths like honesty is the best policy, do unto others as you would have them do unto you, and never talk badly about someone else or misjudge another—unless, as the Dakota Sioux Indian prayer says, "you have walked in his moccasins for two weeks." If they had nothing good to say about someone, generally they would say nothing. They were stoic, strong, and principled. At the same time, they were quiet and gentle people.

Dad was faithful to friends. So faithful that, when his pheasant-hunting friend died an early and unexpected death, my dad felt that he couldn't hunt anymore: his friend couldn't hunt, so neither could he. Right or wrong, it was his sense of principled fidelity to a dear friend.

My mother was a special confidant for my dad throughout their nearly fifty years of marriage. But she was also a special confidant to the two other "men" in her life, distinctively different in her relationship with each son—loving each as very special parts of her life.

One of my finest memories came as a young boy of five on a cold early April evening in 1947. Henry Ford had just died. Henry Ford's company had provided employment for my grandfather. So my dad wanted my brother and me to be with him as he paid his respects to this giant of Detroit and American history, a man who had made life possible for his immigrant parents and himself. He held my twelve-year-old brother's hand and alternated holding mine with holding me in his arms so that the three of us in an interminably long line at the Dearborn Rotunda could pass by the bier of this industrial scion. I remember his telling me how important this man was to us. I've never forgotten the lesson of fidelity in this simple gesture of my father with his two sons.

Needless to say, my father was unbelievably proud when I took an assignment at Ford headquarters thirty years later, a few years after I resigned the priesthood. He would salute as he drove by the headquarters building, say-ing to himself, "My son works there." I am sure that he relived the days of his youth with an immigrant father who fulfilled his dreams not far from where his own son now worked. Whenever I had a chance, I would leave my office on the second floor of the headquarters and find reason to visit the Dearborn Rouge Plant, where my grandfather had worked in the maintenance department. For me, this was where the real Ford men were. I would do this at least once a month, and I would stop to talk with workers there, remembering a grandfather whom I never knew. Somehow, his spirit lived with me when I visited the Rouge.

At the heart of the family were Frank and Margaret (Girard) Josaitis. Their lives were exemplary, but not easy. She was a full-time homemaker and he a dedicated meat-cutter for forty-six years, all but the first four of them with the Kroger Company. Each had continued the dynasty of their immigrant parents, continuing their dreams of a wonderful life in urban Detroit and, eventually, suburban Lincoln Park. For them, their two sons, Norman and Marvin, represented their contribution to the making of family in twentieth century America. They, in their fading years, never ceased to support their sons and were proud to see each become Catholic priests and each attain several academic honors, including doctorate degrees. In my own mind their dedication to family, work, and principled living earned each an honorary degree. They were equally proud when each son decided for various reasons to change vocational directions and careers when that time came.

Overview

Beginning in September 1955, I began to mirror the same direction that my brother had taken six years earlier. Educated in a Catholic parochial school in Melvindale, Michigan, for elementary school, I applied to Sacred Heart Seminary High School in Detroit. I traveled an hour by public city buses to the high school seminary the first four of twelve years, designed to mold boys into Catholic priests. Our school had classes six days a week, Monday through Saturday.

In September 1959, I began the next four years at the same seminary college as a boarding student, majoring in philosophy with a minor in English, and moved four years closer to the goal: the Catholic priesthood. No more buses six days per week. The gothic towered college seminary became my home nine months of the year, full-time with only periodic vacations home to my family. I was being educated and fully socialized for my future life as a Catholic priest. A total male environment with little outside encounters and much discipline ensued.

In June 1963, I received my baccalaureate liberal arts degree and was recommended to St. John's Theological Seminary in Plymouth, Michigan, for the final four years of theological studies and preparation. There, in conjunction with the University of Detroit, I received a master's degree in religious studies. Four years later, shortly after the conclusion of Vatican II (the Second Vatican Council, 1962–65), which had convened prelates from around the world to revisit and reform Catholic devotion and thought, I concluded my theological education and priestly formation.

In June 1967, I was ordained a priest for the Catholic Archdiocese of Detroit and began my ministry at St. Michael's Parish in Monroe, Michigan.

In June 1969, I took leave of my parish assignment and left the priesthood.

Thirty years later, I wrote most of the chapters of the book which follow. I set them aside for over ten years in my briefcase, telling myself that I would re-read them in a decade to determine whether I had accurately written what indeed had transpired in seminary and priesthood that caused my gradual distancing from the priesthood and, ultimately, from the Church.

The Night before Ordination

The seminary was still.

Midnight had come and gone.

Morning of the first Saturday in June 1967, ordination Saturday in the diocese, embodied the stillness. Within ten hours the cathedral would echo Latin chants, with some English interspersed. Ablaze with candles, the Tudor pseudo-Romanesque Gothic vault scented with incense and oils would release twenty-eight newly anointed men (eighteen for the Archdiocese of Detroit) as Latin Rite priests to the awaiting Catholic faithful—men "ordained forever according to the order of Melchisedech."[2]

The seminary was still. Dark. 2:00 a.m. The prior evening presented the last opportunity to discuss the past twelve years of study: four years of high school seminary followed by four years of college seminary followed by four years of theological seminary. That evening's discussions intermixed reminiscences of these past twelve years with fears, trepidation, and excitement for the priestly years commencing early next morning. Were we doing the right thing? Should we go through with it? Were any of us worthy? Could celibacy be that rewarding and meaningful? Would we serve God and His people well? The questions and discussions went on and on that evening…and on and on, in some cases, past the stroke of twelve o'clock midnight.

Sleep for most of the young men began sometime just after midnight. Usually, in seminary, a grand silence was enforced and kept from 10:00 p.m. until breakfast. No one was allowed to speak or gesture to anyone else during that period. That practice was suspended the night before ordination. This was the only night of the year that grand silence started later than usual and, in fact, didn't really exist. It was over now. Private bedroom doors, usually bolted, were left unlocked for fear of oversleeping. This was the known custom on ordination eve.

Many former priests and even bishops would visit to chat and spend the evening with the men who had finally reached this hour. After years of study, years of prayer, years of soul-searching, these men had finally reached and attained their goal. The moment of victory was upon the doorstep. "Knock when you awake tomorrow. If I don't call out, come in and wake me up…I don't want to be late on my ordination day." And so friends promised one another. A trusted friend, Blake, and I promised to make sure that neither overslept.

We were mid-twenty-year-old (and a few older) friends for four, eight, twelve years. Bonded friends, closer than blood brothers in some cases: seminarians now, deacons now, but future priests…tomorrow.

An Uninvited Guest

The seminary was still. Dark. 3:00 a.m. No sounds.

The handle carefully, deliberately, quietly released the catch, and the door opened. "Good. He left his door unlocked, as is the custom the night before," the older man whispered to himself. Easy to find the bed in the dark, each room a carbon copy of the other. Warm June nights made seductive entry easy: no blankets, just a sheet. His hand slipped under the white sheet. "White for virginal purity and cleanliness," he continued mumbling to himself. The hand touched the pubic hairs ever so softly and beckoned to caress the silky feel on its way to other places. "Another virgin for Christ, another celibate," he whispered, "just like me."

Blake stirred and rolled. As deep sleep vanished, he felt the hand groping and stroking. "What the . . . " The figure darted quickly toward the door of the room. Blake's eyes opened, catching the light from the corridor peering in through a door opening. And the figure, fleeing in the dim light, faltering to exit unseen, turned his head, profiled and perfectly framed in the entering light. The corridor light identified the intruder. The bishop fled.

Blake charged the door, half asleep, to catch his uninvited guest, but in vain. The bishop had exited the stairwell, whose door clicked shut as a tired Blake reached the corridor.

The seminary was still. Dark.

The remaining hours to dawn were sleepless ones for Blake. His mind flashed scene after scene. His heart raced and pulsed beyond recreation speed. *A bishop in my room. A bishop fondling me! Why me? Had he gotten into the wrong room? Did he intend another and was surprised when he realized his error? What's this all about? What am I getting myself into? Do I report this to the rector … or better still, to the Archbishop? Do I go on with my own ordination? What about my family, all ready and excited after twelve years of support? Twelve years—high school, college, and theological seminary, and ready now for a celebration! What will they think? What will they think? A bishop! They'll think that I'm hallucinating. My family will be disgraced. But then, the ethics and moral questions. I need to report this event, don't I? I need to whistle blow, don't I? If this happened to me, were there others? Were there others even tonight? Does this bishop always do this? Did he mistakenly come into my room rather than someone else's? Is this an omen for me?*

Blake slept no more.

The silence of night was broken only by a heavy heartbeat and cascading tears. A bishop!

Soul-searching at Dawn

When I heard the knock at dawn, I expected that some-one—probably Blake—would be all aglow. Today, we would become priests after twelve years of planning, studying, praying, struggling, and searching. As planned the night before, a six o'clock rap at my door signaled that Blake was ready to breakfast with me and chat about our ordination to the priesthood, five hours away.

"Thanks, Blake"—I ventured through the cracked door—"see you at breakfast."

"No, Marv, please get ready quickly and meet me outside. I need to talk before breakfast."

I opened the door more fully. "What's wrong, Blake? You look terrible."

"Marv, we need to talk," he whispered. His voice cracked under the strain.

The story of a bishop's early morning assault on Blake floored me with surprise, remorse, shock, maybe even shame. Blake was one of the most ethical persons I knew and have known. Coming from a strong family, his ethnic brand of Catholicism was hewn by Kantian imperatives, definitively rigid and universal moral principles with few grays, if any… black/white ethics, right/wrong behaviors, good/bad, and virtue always contrasted with sin.

"I need to report the bishop to the authorities, Marv," he cried. Blake felt the right thing to do was report the incident to the ecclesiastical authorities, even the Archbishop. "I have a moral obligation, even if it means that he will refuse to ordain me today." My friend struggled with honesty beyond reproach.

We talked. We didn't have that much time. After ninety minutes, we painfully concluded that the 1967 Catholic Church was not ready to fairly and equitably process this painful truth about one of its "princes."

"Blake, who will believe you?" I ventured. "You will be held back from ordination today by a rector and an archbishop questioning your motives and maybe even your sexual maturity or, worse yet, your sexual orientation. Like a man raped, you will become an ecclesiastical victim. Church authorities will protect the bishop, not you. I beg you to remain silent, become ordained, and hope that the bishop will grieve his egregious wrongdoing and come forward himself. And, Blake, I will remain silent so long as you want me to. Don't forget our training, our drenching of training about confessional secrecy."

Blake listened. We prayed together.

Right or wrong, we agreed that Blake should remain quiet about it, be ordained, and go on with his life as a priest. There were no witnesses. It would be his word against a bishop; the Church system would protect the latter and punish the former. We realized that Blake would be the one to suffer and—more so—Blake's family, who were preparing as we spoke for their trip (anticipated for twelve years) to the cathedral.

Blake and I had been through these years of adolescence and early manhood together, joys and sorrow together. Unbelievably strange life experiences transpired in seminary life and discipline: suicidal classmates, homosexual classmates ushered away silently, severe punishment inflicted on anyone daring to question either seminary or clerical authority, intense homophobic attitudes, and mistrust of women as "products of Eve," to name a few. And now this unimaginable event as we were concluding our seminary life.

In our naiveté, we hoped that the bishop would be faithful to the same code of honor that we had lived by. In our naiveté, we hoped that the bishop would be faithful to the moral code that we treasured. This never happened. To this day, Blake and I wonder whether there were other victims, clerical or lay, at the hands of this bishop or whether this was a one night failing. Blake and I were ordained priests later that morning, with a bishop's secret buried deeply within the depths of our psyche and spirit.

Four Decades Later

After over forty years, the grand silence is broken, and now shared in an attempt to add more insight into a church struggling with sexual wounds that are, in the words of Eugene Kennedy (himself a former priest), "unhealed." Over forty years have passed with a bishop's secret moment kept—like a confessional secret—between friends, once brother priests.

I proffer that the unhealed wound of the Church never was totally healed within the bishop; otherwise, he would have encountered his victim directly at some time and would have asked for forgiveness. The bishop, too, kept the secret, unless he acted as so many Catholics do, thinking that a quick private absolution in a confessional rights the wrong. Hopefully, he never replicated the act, although he never apologized nor acknowledged his shame to Blake. Maybe he was never ashamed. Bishops, more so even than priests, have a tendency to view themselves above the law, much like some CEOs and executives today, some of whom I have met and worked for as well.

Little did the bishop know how his act that ordination morning was another moment of truth moving me away from the priesthood that I was about to enter.

After forty-plus years, the grand silence is broken. Broken because of the current pedophilia and sexual misconduct of clergy finally becoming public. The clerical sexual problem, however, is deeper than people—especially the hierarchy—admit.

The problem is a Catholic systemic one of monumental proportions, fostered in practices as well as theological teachings, which require an overhauling. The silence is broken because this former priest and former Catholic does not want to see the Church continue to bury the sickness by writing off the problem to a few scapegoats. Many teachings of the Church and the mythology that surrounds them may be the sources that continue to foster psychic wounds and immature behavior in the larger-than-life communities of believers. A few "really troubled" individuals emerge. But they are the proverbial tip of the iceberg.

My credentials for objective comment are enhanced by four decades of freeing myself from the emotional, psychological, social, and philosophical shackles of a Church, which formed me. The paradigm shifts that I have made throughout my life, prior to the priesthood and after, began as a philosophy undergraduate. The process, once begun, deepened as a theology student through analytical criticism, matured through two years as a priest, and evolved over four decades as a college/university professor, business executive, Realtor, pianist, counselor, author, husband, father, and grandfather. An additional few years as an Episcopalian and vestryperson in two Episcopal parishes shed yet another different light on organized religious constructs. Several decades of being "un-churched" have done the same. I can look back critically and unemotionally now. And I will.

My ideal hope is that even one person will find a root or a spark of meaning that leads to a personal metamorphosis and human growth—like my own—based on a new set of paradigms, unlikely to be found in *any* organized religious system today.

My Promise at Ordination

As I lay prostrate on the terrazzo stone and marble flooring of the cathedral that morning in 1967, whilst the litany of the saints was chanted and prayed, I decided that my priesthood would last only so long as I truly felt that I could make a difference. As the chant echoed throughout the nave, I told God that if I ever felt that to remain a priest may mean compromising my ideals as so many priests had done (with now an addition of a bishop), I would resign. If I ever suspected that I could become a priest who was lonely, derelict, perhaps alcoholic, devoid of human warmth, officious, unfaithful to principles, wrapped up in administration rather than mission, intellectually dishonest, theologically compromised, I told God that I would resign. Two years later, I did just that.

Strange as it may seem, my movement away from the priesthood began six years before I was ordained. Severe paradigm shifts started occurring during my mid-college undergraduate years.

Prior to age twenty, my classmates thought that I might be sent, like my brother before me, to study theology in Rome. This was usually considered a sign of ecclesiastical high potentiality. My academic standing was high, my obedience to seminary regimen was consistent, and my Catholic belief system purist and traditional. During my last years of college, however, this traditionalist began to expose himself to a non-traditional, questioning, intellectually challenging world. By the end of my baccalaureate, I began to slowly re-fashion the belief system I had taken relatively unchallenged as absolute truth. A paradigmatic shift away from traditional Catholicism and eventually Catholicism itself was occurring.

Importance
of Paradigms

Paradigms are those mental constructs that allow us to perceive reality a certain way and fashion our behavior in kind. They are the most powerful substratum of our lives. These mental frameworks explain why men behave and think the way that they do. At the same time, they can be liberating and/or confining. The Magna Charta, Galileo's insights, Newtonian physics, the Divine Right of Kings, the French Revolution, the industrial revolution, the emergence of Jeffersonian democracy are all defining moments that explain shifts in the way people view reality. Change doesn't occur unless basic thought constructs are altered. All of the above historical references could not have occurred unless there was a paradigmatic change at the time, which made it possible for a new vision.

The changing way to perceive things actually permits a person and persons to alter behavior. Men act on belief systems until they have a different set of mental constructs that will guide them to think and behave differently. A paradigm must be replaced by another mindset in order to permit a change in human behavior.

For me, significant paradigmatic changes slowly emerged as I read every existentialist philosopher and writer I could in the early 1960s: Sartre, Camus, de Beauvoir, Rand, Kierkegaard, Marcel, and other atheistic or religious counterparts. Throughout college I re-read Thoreau and the transcendentalists as well as C.S. Lewis.

While I had to study and regurgitate Thomas Aquinas and scholastic philosophy with half my tests performed in Latin, my heart and spirit were moving away from Aquinas and "official" Church teaching. I remember supporting therapeutic abortion on an ethics test (taken in Latin) in 1962. My priest professor gave me the lowest grade that I had ever received on a test, writing back to this usually "A" student that "abortion under any circumstances was unjustified—that I had better re-study." He had failed to allow me to logically take a position contra-Rome, contra-scholasticism in a philosophy class. The moment was defining for me: I was being asked to memorize, not think.

Later in 1962, I wrote a philosophy paper on existentialism as a term paper in History of Philosophy. A second priest professor praised my writing and research, but cautioned that I was dealing with ideas that may cause conflict with Catholic theology—"Please be careful," he cautioned, despite the "A-" grade. That priest whom I always respected eventually left the clergy himself.

A third priest professor called me into his office when I had written an essay in a creative writing class about a young man who, in discovering himself, had encountered a young lady in a bar and later in bed. The essay, one of my favorite productions that semester, kept me from receiving anything but "B" grades because "seminarians should not write, let alone think about such topics."

A fourth priest called me and another classmate friend on the carpet when he discovered that we two twenty-one-year-olds had been picked up on a holiday by the biological sister and female cousin of my friend (both in their mid-late twenties, by the way) for a five-hour trip to visit elderly relatives. We were putting ourselves into potential sin since, as he asserted: "Even blessed candles burn." The fact that we were picked up in a red convertible by two women could create "grave scandal within the community."

Moving in a New Direction

As I graduated from college, my trusted faculty advisor, with tears in his eyes, informed me that the faculty wanted to send me to Rome, but a few faculty members were concerned that I was becoming a bit of a free thinker with too free a spirit. A decision was made, therefore, that despite my high academic standing, high character, and commendable behavior throughout my eight years in the seminary high school and college, the faculty feared that Rome was not as appropriate for me as the local theology school. My trusted advisor, a wonderfully human *monsignor,* had the tears, but I didn't. As I left his office, thanking him for his candor and openness, I lifted my palm up and internally shouted: *Yes!*

My parents had spent four years waiting for the return of their first-born from Rome. I had always feared that I could be asked to replicate yet another four years of agonized waiting and longing in the hearts of the most beautiful people I knew and loved. I had also lived in the shadow of an older brother, often being confronted with the speculation that I merely was following his lead and was not my own person. Once in high school, a priest who had taught both of us shouted at me in class that my brother would not have behaved that way. I quickly retorted, "I am not my brother." For some reason, this experience was never encountered again, but deep down I think that I always feared its public re-emergence. And finally, I knew that I was moving away from Catholic orthodoxy and feared that Rome might make it impossible for me to continue the journey. Hence, I shouted for joy internally at the news that I was domestic-bound for the next four years. How fortunate I felt that I was! The philosophical shift occurring slowly within me would blossom during the next four years at an American theological seminary.

Life in a Traditional Seminary

The priests who had taught and mentored me in high school and college had their idiosyncrasies, but generally they were healthy adult men. On the other hand, the theological faculty had more than its share of neuroses, psychoses, retentive behavior, and immaturity. And they wielded massive power in determining whether a candidate for priesthood would continue to ordination or be "clipped" temporarily or permanently "eliminated" along the way.

These were our mentors and teachers for the next four years: a couple of self-proclaimed mystics, a closet homosexual with soppy ideas and fawning behavior, a couple of priests recovering from mental breakdowns, an arrogant socialite from the East Coast who flaunted his haut-couture upbringing and insulted anyone from other parts of the country whom he felt inferior (which included most of us), a couple of nervous and twitching delicate men, and a couple of recovering alcoholics who actually were rated highest among all of us for their human qualities and adult behavior. In their midst were a few truly well-balanced individuals, including the recovering alcoholics, who sought their own refuge with the outside world of parishioners they served part-time and not their own colleagues…a few even moving in different paradigmatic directions than Mother Church.

For the most part, moral theology was taught from thirteenth century scholastic premises: dogmatic theology was Baltimore Catechism elevated to the graduate school. Canon law was king, routing the spirit out of faith in the worst of legalistic machinations. Liturgy was monastic. Sermon preparation was nothing more than speech elocution. Sacramental theology was pious, symbolic, saccharine thought.

The seminary was run like a monastery around the breviary and grand silence was a good part of the evening and morning. Morning began with Matins—sleepy(ing) men in silence, meeting for prayer and meditation before dawn, followed by the liturgy (still in Latin). Silence could be broken only at breakfast. Morning classes ended with prayer at noon. Lunch at assigned tables was partially social and partially silent as ten to fifteen minutes of reading from the *Martyrology* and/or the *Dark Night of the Soul* occurred alternately to a silent and disbelieving student body. We thought most of the readings were pious and maybe even fictitious, but we endured them. The faculty sat above the students on a dais in the dining room, as they did in the classrooms. These were their security/authoritative perches. Afternoon classes commenced, followed by recreational time, prayer in the chapel at six, dinner (again partially silent), free time until ten...and then: *grand silence.* No one could speak until breakfast the next day. Residence halls and private bedrooms were always silent places with no mingling or room exchange *ever* permitted, with one exception—the night before ordination.

And such was the training for the next four years to prepare *men* to be parish *priests.* The glove and the hand didn't match, but it was traditional and unchangeable. Black capes, black cassocks (robes), and black birettas (ecclesiastical caps formerly worn by clergy) were the dress code except when free time or recreation time was scheduled.

Attempting to Change Seminary Life

During my second year, I decided on my own to take a formal survey of students on changes needed at our major seminary. With some trepidation, I presented my unsolicited findings to the priests in charge on December 3, 1965, pondering whether they would consider me a less worthy Martin Luther posting a new version of the ninety-five theses at the Wittenberg Chapel. To my surprise, they accepted this critical analysis of students' feelings and demands; they read and debated its conclusions. I had purposely framed the document within the spirit of the Second Vatican Council, a breath of fresh air within the Catholic Church aimed at modernizing and restoring life to a static institution.

Slowly, the teaching faculty allowed some changes to occur. A growing number of students, however, demanded revolutionary alterations to life as we knew it in this major theological seminary and were not satisfied with the slower speed comfortable to the more traditional group of Sulpician priests (belonging to the order of St. Sulpice) who taught at this seminary. The student body gathered at times in protest at the continuation of a more monastic regimen.

By the end of my third year, obviously now aware of the unrest brewing, the Archdiocese secured a number of replacements for the priests who were unnerved by the student criticisms and protests. The new priests on the faculty were more progressive in their thoughts and were more open to mature dialogue. However, those students who had been less diplomatic than I were either "clipped" temporarily from further advancements or permanently dismissed. A few left voluntarily. For some unknown reason, I was unable to make the decision to "call it quits."

My diplomacy was a cover-up for the in-depth dislike I had for the system as well as the Church as it existed. I was committed and driven to try to make a difference in altering that status from within as a priest. I decided to become part of the solution. While I continued to walk a careful line on exams, I fed back or even regurgitated "Church-think" without totally being unfaithful to myself and my thoughts. My reading and private study took me into the worlds beyond the existentialists whom I had discovered a few years earlier. I now devoured the nouveau thought of Vatican II by reading Rahner, Schillibecks, de Chardin, Merton, and anyone attempting to move away from scholastic theology. Pope John XXIII, to the dismay of our theological instructors, had helped to bring fresh air into the Church. There was *hope.*

Former mindsets, I thought, were being replaced with newer, more dynamic constructs. This permitted me as well as the majority of my friends to continue on our pursuit of priesthood. Idealists as we were, we thought that the world—the Catholic world—was waiting breathlessly for a new style priest. Later, we would discover that a chasm was emerging between our thoughts and those of the majority of people in the pew who were still imbued with traditional teachings. The newer theological writings that I was assessing were all helping to shape me positively from negative past experiences. I determined to be as far away as I could from the pitiful specimens of humanity still on the teaching faculty and the pious medieval spirituality they espoused. I determined to interpret Church beliefs through reason and logic as much as I could.

One of my friends and classmate privately warned me that I was becoming heretical. Not surprisingly, he was one of a handful ordained with me who still continues as a priest. He chastised me because I supported artificial birth control as well as abortion and divorce under certain circumstances. Because I accepted most of the issues raised by sixteenth century reformers such as Martin Luther, he was concerned about my salvation. And the list of disagreements with other Church teachings gave him further justification to call me a heretic. I believed that it was the total community of believers who actually consecrated bread and wine at Mass through the hands and voice of their priest representative. I believed as the Episcopalians did that all believers could eat at the LORD's table. I disagreed with the Church's position on indulgences, Marian theology and dogma, the role of women in the Church, the meaning of prayer, the meaning of sin, the way in which sexuality was so preeminently geared to guilt, the doctrine of original sin as developed by St. Augustine, and the infallibility of the pope as defined. For all of these positions, he claimed that I was truly a heretic. I was accused of this later as a young priest by some of the older priests with whom I served. Obviously, new paradigms were shaping me and my belief system.

In real life, I carefully shaped my thought so that it revealed a reasoned evolutionary rather than revolutionary pitch. During my fourth and final year in theology as an ordained deacon, I began to evolve a reasoned approach to faith. One of the parish priests I served as a deacon reiterated what I was hearing from my seminary friend: "You have an independent spirit, and you challenge authority in such a way that I fear ultimately for your salvation." He didn't use the word *heretic.*

A New Kind of Priest

When I was ordained, idealism defined my spirit. I was the first newly ordained twenty-five-year-old sent to the southernmost outreaches of the diocese. Places like that were usually reserved for priests who were working out personal problems of one sort or another. My idealism from June 1967 to June 1969 was attacked on many fronts.

My view was that I was sent to a whole community, not just a Catholic community. So during my first few months, I visited every Protestant and Orthodox clergyman in the town, introducing myself and suggesting that we get together in dialogue. There were no synagogues or mosques within forty miles, or I would have included their rabbis and imams as well.

After three months of regular monthly meetings, we became aware that ecumenism was just a word, a popular façade, but not a reality. In effect, Christians still wanted to live on and live out their differences. They wanted their own traditions. And here I had thought that the world was ready for genuine Christianity, "Mere Christianity," in the words of C. S. Lewis. Rather, I discovered that ecumenism was to be relegated to an occasional sharing of a podium at a town meeting or a common prayer said together to show off "unity." But when I mentioned having common services on Sunday or common religion classes or sharing buildings and pulpits, joint marriage services, attendance at another church on a moving cycle in place of one's own church, the cry came from disbelieving clergy of all faiths: "No way, Marv." On some of my theological positions, even one of the Lutheran pastors in town said that he feared that I was heretical. This was quite an interesting twist from a man who traced his belief system back to the great German reformer at the Wittenberg Chapel.

Even today, more than forty years later, I continue to see mankind divided to the point of war over their belief systems. Christians are divided from other Christians. Muslims are divided from other Muslims. Both groups, which are the most proselytizing religious groups in the world, form a trilogy of defiance and tension with Judaism. These three dominant interpreters of religious faith are not even unified within their own worldview. But each religious tradition or traditions claims to have *the* truth, a faith system that they quickly interpret as factual reality. And to others, the word *heretic* is interestingly used. I have felt the sting. Other faith systems throughout the world are too often considered by these three as primitive, superstitious, inferior, or pagan in worshiping false gods. This overwhelming realization that I experienced as a young priest in my failed attempt to bring clergy together from within the Christian forum in one small town was the first peg in my decision to leave the clergy.

I was assigned to the original German parish in a town with three other distinctly original ethnic parish congregations: French, Italian, and Irish. I lived with a priest-pastor who was more than forty years older than I. I call him "Father PRA" since that fits best his demeanor and his activities: Pious, Regimented, Accountant. This Teutonic priest strongly resembled a cherub in size and disposition. For years he had mastered a sweet, pious public persona, often highlighting his cherubic face with uplifted eyes coupling a prayer-gaze with soft folded hands, feigning communion with the divine. The uninitiated easily viewed this as saintly behavior, and older female parishioners and religious members of the community in particular loved the image. I had been duped early on in our relationship to conclude sanctity as well. However, it didn't take me long to experience the rigidly inflexible regimentation that equaled and often exceeded the pious.

PRA masterfully controlled and bossed whomever he could, including parish staff. His favorite easy target was our live-in housekeeper. When I arrived on the scene, she quickly sensed an ally. Her tearful outbreaks at his insensitive barking and belittling waned as I bolstered her coping skills in private conversations with her. PRA eventually seemed displeased that he couldn't twist her feelings quite so easily now.

From day one, PRA never accepted me as an equal but rather required filial devotion and obedience from me. He spent most of his days as an accountant poring over parish financial books in his office, analyzing every penny spent and saved. He expected me to live a quasi-monastic life based on the Roman Breviary of Prayers prescribed at certain times of the day, along with his imposed curfew and rectory regimentation. He sought no input from me on any parish issues or plans.

I revolted.

I was never given a key to the church, the elementary school, or the rectory, which was supposed to be my home. The old pastor set 10:00 p.m. as a curfew for this twenty-five-year-old. When I broke this curfew during the first week of living together, he angrily opened the door as I rang the bell at 11:30 p.m. I warned him that I would ax down the door if he ever dared to lock it after 10:00 p.m. again. I got a key the next day.

We lived a cold war during my two years as a priest. I was relegated to have Mass at 6:00 a.m. every morning and rarely with the school children at 8:00 a.m., because I was "introducing them to too many new ideas—even having them talking out loud and having fun in church." My 6:00 a.m. congregation was a few seventy-year-old women who sat in the back row and wouldn't participate beyond the rattling of their rosaries. But they were mine—and I tried to change their perceptions and ideas slowly. I succeeded, minimally. Fortunately, others started to come on their way to work, and I introduced them to a new spirit of Catholicism. But it was painful. I wanted to have an evening Mass. I was allowed, but infrequently. I became a "Mass" machine for these 6:00 a.m. few traditionalists.

When I asked the pastor to consider something else, he denied my request and reminded me that I only earned $75.00 a month salary with room and board. In addition, he paid me a stipend of $3.00 for every Mass that I celebrated during the month. This was 60 percent of the required donation, which parishioners gave to have someone in their family, usually a deceased person, remembered specifically during that Mass. The list was published each week. I hated the system but buckled economically. My meager monthly salary was enough to handle my basic car expenses, but I had no other source of possible income other than the Mass routine. In our diocese, the tradition had developed that the Christmas collection went to the pastor as a thank-you supplementary income. Most pastors, then, typically shared this with their associate priests. Mine gave me $50.00 as a Christmas present. When asked to go on a vacation with some of my priest friends, they didn't realize at the time when I declined that I was being kept hostage by an older traditionalist trying to model me according to his fashion. The monastic seminary life was still with me. But I couldn't afford to escape what I was learning to dislike.

As a consequence, I started to have regular "home" Masses in the evening for some of those who were receptive to a new type of Catholicism. Eight or ten of us would sit around a kitchen or dining room table reverently, with no special ecclesiastical garb, with bread made by the welcoming family, and we would celebrate the liturgy together. For me, this was the way it was meant to be. Instead of a sermon, we would have a discussion. I found this extremely satisfying. Nonetheless, I learned to hate my inability to have a reasonable boss and live what I thought a young priest deserved.

One of the first things that I demanded was the installation of drapes on my confessional door and the pastor's confessional door. The two confessionals faced one another on opposite sides of the church's nave. The pastor had left the door screen on each open so that the priest sitting inside could see who walked in and out of the confessional. I think that he left them open so that he could see who confessed to me rather than to him. After much argumentation, he agreed to have our maintenance man install light purple drapes over each door.

Many of my penitents came to me crying after the old pastor in the confessional across the aisle had shouted at them. My pulpit became the confessional where I treated "sins of the flesh" as minor when compared to failing to communicate with one's spouse, hurting someone you loved with a nasty word or unjust anger, lying, or disrespect in any form. I later found out that some of the little children's parents eventually pushed them into the pastor's confessional because they wanted their children to be influenced by a harsh tone telling them they were wrong and that God was unhappy with them. These parents didn't want their small children leaving the confessional smiling and skipping as so many others did from confessing to Father Jo.

I wanted to introduce a community "group" penance experience rather than the individual confessional. It took me nearly two years, but the older priests and traditional Catholics weren't as supportive as I thought they would be. I couldn't help thinking that most priests in the community feared their "power" in the confessional waning, and the traditionalists feared that "guilt" was being given a new lease on life. They couldn't stand the idea that I and others like me (there were two other priests in town who supported change) were trying to bring people up in the Church differently than they were raised and that they expected be continued.

The nun who was principal at our elementary school was a religious disciplinarian, classic Hollywood-style, a self-proclaimed protector of Church law and order in her core. Her stern, unsmiling demeanor usually was coupled with folded arms and a firmly set jaw. Despite her self-perceived exalted station in life, she occasionally accommodated a selected passerby with her forced smile. Realizing her human failing, she would just as quickly cast her eyes downward and assume her former proper religious decorum. A sister of the old order despite her four decades, she had concluded within four months of my arrival that I would ruin discipline and proper Church behavior for her entrusted elementary school minions when I chatted with the kids at Mass encouraging their dialogue rather than preaching Church teachings at them. Consequently, she insisted with PRA that I had to be relegated to the 6:00 a.m. Mass attended by a small crowd of rosary bead rattling elder members of the community huddled in the back pew. I would be permitted to celebrate the 8:00 a.m. children's Mass only when the pastor was on vacation. She assured PRA that she would report back my conduct when he returned. She knew that I knew that she would ... something like that!

The nun principal also supported the old pastor in keeping me away from the classrooms where I was clearly unfit to enter due to my unwillingness to reinforce a negative joyless theology based on sin, sin, and more sin. I thought that Rome had crumbled the day that I indicated my strong preference to have the first communion class of second graders skip any introduction to the confessional at that early age! That sealed my fate: I would definitely be relegated to contact with the children only on the playground during recess time, and not in the classroom. The kids would run when they saw me, give me hugs, and tell me about their day in school. I caught her frowning with pursed lips more than once whenever she saw this recess warmth and childlike affection for their young "Father Jo." I tried not to show my sadness and my anger at the total educational deprivation that was now inflicted upon me in my first parish.

During my first six months, the pastor brought in a traditionalist Catholic physician to talk to parents about teaching their children the "sins of the flesh." I challenged him publicly when he proposed the traditional moral stand on masturbation, pre-marital sex leading to marriage commitment, and artificial birth control. I thought that I would get support—maybe even cheers—from the parishioners attending the meeting. Instead, I found that the strong majority were traditionalists who wanted their children taught the way that they had been taught. They were afraid that if priests did not reinforce guilt on sexual issues, then they would lose control of their children and the devil would take over. During my two years, I refused to teach any course on sexuality if it meant teaching traditional Catholic thought. I never was asked to teach such a course.

I began to wear a tie and regular men's clothes more than the clerical collar and cassock. I frequented a pub called the "Rathskeller" in town at night and chatted with folks of all types, whether they were respected in town or not. The waitress, Mary Lou, usually put a quarter in the jukebox to play Louis Armstrong's "It's a Wonderful World" as I entered the downstairs cave. If she didn't, I did. I always sat with a glass of ginger ale. The pastor and his traditionalists were shocked. After all, "a priest should not be found associating with sinners," I was told. I questioned their insensitivity and misplaced moral judgments. To this day I still continue to have difficulty understanding how these critics could marry their words with truly Christian principles of love.

Everything I did during those two years was intended to bring human reality into the world of the unreal. Regular church people wanted—indeed, expected—their priests to be something other than human. They placed their priests on pedestals and expected that, as they paid their dues, the priest would say what they wanted him to say and act as they wanted him to act. I was beginning to be criticized by the traditionalists who even wrote to the Archbishop regarding my attire (including wearing shorts when I bicycled or golfed on my day off); my lack of complete obedience to the pastor; some of my beliefs and interpretation of Church teaching (i.e. heaven and hell are not necessarily "places" but rather "states" of being); the fact that I wore a simple silver wedding band (for me a symbol of my dedication to the people); my instances of inviting non-Catholics to receive communion at weddings, funerals, and other gatherings; giving Communion under both species (bread and wine)…the list goes on and on.

The Archbishop didn't call me in, but he asked one of his auxiliary bishops to do so. My discussion with the auxiliary bishop by the time that it was arranged was focused on the fact that I had decided to resign. I could no longer be faithful to myself and the paradigmatic shift that had transformed me. Nor would I decide to become another official reformer outside the Church. I had decided to transform only those worlds that I could touch and affect in a different and meaningful way. I decided not to create a soapbox alternative lifestyle.

Resigning from the Priesthood

Besides the crucifixion of my idealism that came from the majority of laity opposed to paradigmatic change within, the final leg of my idealistic shattering came from the hands of the clergy (exceptions being my two close, but slightly older, priest associates in the neighboring parishes of the same town) and from the Archbishop himself. Throughout my life, a preeminence of principle—logically reasoned principle as well as intuitively resolved principle—always has been paramount.

During my theological studies, which included one year as an ordained deacon working in parishes, I began to experience a clergy that was unfaithful to these ideals, men who lived a double standard. There was the pastor who made advances on altar boys, and, believe it or not, a pastor who physically examined young couples seeking marriage to make sure that they were definitively male and female. How he got away with this baffled another priest friend and I who were in disbelief at the unquestioning trust and blind faith innocent people willingly placed in their priests.

Sixteen months after ordination, I attended a retreat with thirty other priests. I was shocked to discover that only one other priest there was happy remaining in the priesthood. I wasn't letting my frustrations get the better of me. I was still truly happy, although challenged beyond belief.

Twenty-eight of the thirty admitted that, if they were younger and knew what to do with their lives, they would leave the priesthood. This was crushing to my idealism. So too was the awareness openly discussed at the retreat that a few priests also had extramarital affairs, secretive and regular consorts or dates, dual-standard vacations where anything went, "closet" homosexual behaviors and encounters, or other convenient relationships. One priest at the retreat eventually suffered the ignominy of death at the hands of his sexual prey. Two priests in attendance offered to set me up with a list of "safe" restaurants and other places where I could go to experience the "reality" of life. While these priests lived a lie under anybody's assessment, nonetheless they seemed to have convinced themselves that their behaviors were justified.

I became aware of other priests who politicked to get "plum" parishes where their income could escalate immensely and "plum" assignments for self-aggrandizement. Many priests became "administrators" rather than shepherds; some became brick-and-mortar aces. Others drank alcohol unbelievably. Gatherings of priests, even around religious events, were evenings of the best scotch and the braggadocios about their prowess and wealth. Many were heavy drinkers—some, alcoholics. I saw trapped older priests wanting out but not having the paradigmatic framework that permitted them that freedom.

And the Archbishop, as much a giant theologically and liturgically that he was in the Vatican II movement, was not able to go any further than he did to encourage change. Like many bishops even up to the present, he reassigned "problem" priests to less populated areas. By so doing, he continued to protect the illness within the clergy rather than decidedly addressing the anomalies head-on. Probably a victim of Roman "politics of the possible," he told a meeting of over one hundred of us priests in early 1969 that certain Church teachings, such as those on artificial contraception and indulgences, had to be publicly upheld, but what we did to support individual conscience privately, especially in the confessional, was our choice.

As much as I admired the man who ordained me, when I met with him in 1969 to tell him of my decision to resign, he offered to reassign me anywhere, even to a university where my ideas and beliefs would reach a receptive enlightened audience. On the face of it, this was a remarkable offer, an open offer. At the time, I pointed out my theological and moral dilemma. I clicked off my reasons for resigning (which did not include celibacy *per se,* since I didn't leave the priesthood specifically to marry), but did include his failure to stand up and be counted on major issues being debated. I told him that he was being hypocritical in letting the front-line priests work things out in the privacy of the confessional. I even went so far to indicate that he was hypocritical in reassigning people like me to live in forums where a small group could "experiment" with new ideas and practices off the beaten track while he upheld publicly the outmoded belief systems and policies of a Roman Curia. I told him that he was being, in all due respect, intellectually dishonest in pretending to look the other way, even protecting the sexual misbehavior of many of his priests. Later, the Archbishop's personal priest secretary told me that I shouldn't have told the Archbishop that he was intellectually dishonest. It hurt him. I considered it "tough love."

My Farewell

Two years to the date that I had become associate pastor, I was preaching at every Mass, explaining to parishioners my decision to leave them and pursue a different career. I would remain serving the community at large and its youth in particular by joining the faculty at the local college, teaching philosophy and English at the undergraduate level. My last words were all positive and laudatory. I thanked them for the opportunity to live among them as a priest and looked forward to continuing to live in the community as a professor. The old pastor cried. A few trusted parishioners close to the pastor later confided in me that he had felt guilty; he was concerned that he may have caused this unspeakable event.

Interestingly, the nun principal neither commented on my resignation nor wished me well. I have suspected all these years that she probably feared the influence that I might have on the college students soon to be my new congregation with the community … and I wouldn't be relegated only to the playground anymore!

I found out several years later that the pastor had purged my name from any official church document, whiting out my name and inserting his on baptismal and marriage records—illegal, I am sure. However, I guess that in his own mind, this spared the validity of these acts by removing the infidel's name. He had not yet read Hayaka-wa's concept that the "map is not the territory," the picture or symbol was not the reality.

More parishioners than I would have thought actually wept because I was leaving them. These were my friends—friends of all ages. Some asked me to pastor their "home liturgies" informally. But I refused. Once I left the clergy, I put behind me the robes, the chalice, the books, and the behavior. The only artifact of this part of my life that I still have is the silver cup I purchased on a trip to Disney-land for $25.00, which I thought befitting to use as the chalice of a poor, small town, bumpkin priest. It was part of my honest past and wouldn't become part of a dishon-est future except as a relic still housed in our dining room china cabinet. I was leaving on philosophical and theo-logical grounds with paradigms much different than those required to remain a priest in the Catholic Church of 1969.

That summer I attended Catholic liturgy as a layman a handful of times, only to realize that too many priests and congregations had lost the spirit and meaning of beauti-ful, meaningful liturgy: they were going through motions, fulfilling an obligation to be in church. As a priest, I gave my all to make sure that the liturgy was meaningful and beautiful; this was paramount to my ministry. My involve-ment with the Church was hanging now by a thread.

New Beginnings

I began to date and dance for the first time in my life. The former was forbidden of seminarians, and I had been obedient to the rule. Some of my former seminary classmates had not followed this prescript; had they been discovered or reported, they may have been expelled from the seminary. The closest that I came, albeit innocent, was during a Saturday afternoon break as a college sophomore that I mentioned earlier when another friend and I were picked up by his sister and female cousin (both much older than us) to visit aging relatives of his for the afternoon. When we arrived back to the seminary later that afternoon, we were each called into the office of the college's Spiritual Director, a very kind but prudish priest, who read the riot act to us, indicating the scandal that this behavior of ours caused. He promised to intercede for us this time, but warned that such behavior again could cause immediate dismissal. Eight years later, at age twenty-seven, I found myself with the amorous experiences of a twelve-year-old! I was like an eighth grader attending an adult group dance and party.

During the summer of 1969, I met and dated women for the first time. That summer, on July 5, 1969, I also met the woman of my life on a blind date and dance arranged by one of my former parishioner friends. Our relationship didn't click at first, mostly due to my awkwardness and inexperience, but partially due to a patch she was wearing over an injured eye. More important, I had rarely been alone on a date. At this moment, the wonderful relationships that I had with my mother, a few close female cousins, or a few nun friends didn't really count to help me in this situation.

My experience both in dating and dancing were minimal, at best. Perhaps the word *primitive* describes it more accurately. I had just resigned from the Catholic priesthood a month earlier after having spent twelve faithful "no-dating" years preparing in the seminary. We were in Toledo, Ohio, a quick jaunt from Monroe, where Donna Marie Rimer had lived most of her life and where I would be starting a new career as a community college instructor. What I was experiencing was being alone with a female in a social and potentially amorous relationship for the first time … ever. I had no points of reference. I had no crutches. I didn't know whether it was being "too fast" to even kiss at the end of an evening. Little did either of us expect that on our second date fifteen days later, we would be watching Neil Armstrong's walk on the moon, a symbolic prelude to the marvelous journey we would soon begin ourselves.

My spouse-to-be, whom I waited to kiss after more than two months of dating, gargled mouthwash prior to our getting together because she had begun to worry that this problem was hers. On our first date, the friend that brought us together chastised me for dancing with Donna and holding her like a "piece of liver." While not yet quite a Fred Astaire, I have corrected that observation well over the years with enough ballroom dancing to surprise many people. I still marvel that Donna patiently endured my total innocence or stupidity, whichever was applicable. Our two daughters and daughter-in-law have told their mother that they are not sure they would have endured for as long as she did! Eventually, our relationship clicked.

Exactly three months later on October 5, 1969, we had decided to drive to a lake ninety minutes west of Monroe in what was popularly called the Irish Hills. We stopped there to climb a stately willow tree, a sport that Donna particularly fancied. While we sat in the tree hanging over the shoreline, I handed her a small box. In it was a delicate pearl ring encased in silver.

Donna gasped. "What is this?"

I stammered, "Well, when a guy gives his girl a ring, it usually means that he is asking her to marry him."

A skillful tree climber, Donna nearly fell from the willow! I had just engaged Donna from a willow tree hanging over a pond. She said yes to my marriage proposal, premised on my talking with her parents for their blessing.

Asking Gerald and Ada (Reau) Rimer the simple question was easy. They were the type of informal, Midwestern people who made it easy. The three months of courtship had given me an opportunity to establish a comfortable relationship with two wonderful people, not unlike my own parents. Jerry, as he was called, even resembled my own father, and later often the two of them were asked if they were brothers. Our parents were so similar in interests and values that, after our two families were bonded, the four of them later would even vacation together.

After I asked for their daughter's hand in marriage to a shocked pair, Donna's father excused himself for a private conversation with his daughter. Donna's mother and I made small talk in the meantime. When father and daughter returned to the living room, the bright happy look on their faces told the answer. The affirmative words that followed were unnecessary—but welcomed—by a slightly nervous twenty-seven-year-old engaged young man staring at his slightly nervous twenty-two-year-old fiancée. That evening, October 5, 1969, her mom and dad solidified our future union by accepting me as their new son-to-be.

Six months later, we began our marriage. We celebrate this event every day, a union of best friends who live and have lived an exceptional life together in three countries and three states, always with deep love and trust. Frequently, Donna's anniversary card to me pictures a tree, even a willow tree, as symbolic of that great defining moment together. On our fortieth wedding anniversary, our children and grandchildren presented us with a framed picture created by our eldest child, Kateri, on behalf of all: a willow tree with the appropriate birthstones of each of our then thirteen family members gracing three of its distinct branches. Above the willow tree are the words:

It started in a tree
with a pearl
And look how it's grown
after forty years...

The plaque now graces our dining room buffet center stage, awaiting the addition of a new birthstone for our sixth grandchild and second granddaughter who was born December 6, 2010.

The Final Break
with the Past

Both Catholics when we met, we eventually both left the Church. The odd paradox is that the Church didn't and doesn't yet even recognize our sacrament as holy or valid! Due to our change in mindsets, we do and always have. In life, I guess, one often must define what is important and real from what is superficial and unessential. The little prince in De Saint-Exupery's great classic discovered that often what is essential is invisible to the eye. We clearly have done that.

Because our families were Catholic, we had petitioned the archbishop to marry in the Church, with my only brother—also a priest at the time—officiating at Donna's home parish or her high school chapel in the town where we planned to live and work. The first step was laicization, a convoluted process that revokes the promise of celibacy, a type of annulment as it were, which is made even more difficult because of the Church's belief in the "indelible nature of ordination." I decided to apply for laicization in October 1969.

How naïve I was in taking what appeared to be an honest and straightforward approach. I had forgotten momentarily that the Church is at its heart a major bureaucracy with laws and regulations bent on justifying itself and its rigid interpretations of Christian behavior.

When I arrived at the Chancery office for the Archdiocese of Detroit, a canon lawyer priest of the archdiocese gave me a simple document to sign. There were two justifications to my request for laicization which I needed to admit: first, that I truly had never really wanted to become a priest and wasn't acting freely when I chose to be ordained, and second, that I had a psychological problem that incapacitated me from validly choosing ordination when I did. I was shocked.

In the two-page letter that I had written to Pope Paul VI on October 8, 1969, requesting laicization, I clearly attested to my sound and free choice in becoming a priest and in deciding to leave the clergy. I told the Tribunal priest that the statement he required me to sign was false and contradictory to the letter I had already written to the pope. In actuality, during the twelve years of preparing throughout high school, college, and post-graduate theology seminaries, my behavior and mental health were quite opposite to these statements staring up at me from the paper awaiting my signature.

He smiled and told me that these were just forms created to satisfy an office in Rome; he went on to say that no one doubts my sincerity or health, but that Rome has its ways, and this was just a means to satisfy that bureaucracy. I had forgotten that the bureaucratic Church can be vindictive in humiliating the requestor for clemency. In effect, as one of the first to test the laicization process in the Archdiocese of Detroit, the Church was asking me to submit. I was in disbelief that the Church would demand that I lie in order to be laicized.

The Church believed that I would always be a priest—permanently marked for all eternity. To allow me to marry meant that I had had some mitigating reason that would allow the authorities to "annul," as it were, that event, hence wiping their hands of any ecclesiastical misjudgment in ordaining me in the first place. Now I was expected to falsify my life in order to satisfy their collective conscience. The truth, which makes one free, was not acceptable to the Church. Had I known what the further steps ultimately entailed, I would have left my meeting at the diocesan chancery that day.

When I repeated again to the priest that I couldn't believe that he was asking me to sign my name to a false statement, he replied, "It is just a paper needed to satisfy a Roman cleric. Cross your fingers or toes if you would feel better signing it. Besides, it will allow your families to have a church wedding."

I felt the pressure of the moment—real or imagined—and acted, albeit regrettably, to accommodate a complex situation with a simple signing of a document. The expediency of the moment overtook the principled man I thought I was. Regrettably, I acquiesced and signed the statement. Donna laughed when I told her that I crossed the fingers on my non-writing left hand and tried to cross my toes, but it was difficult.

How wrong I was on that autumn day in 1969. To this day, I wish that I had not signed the artificial laicization papers indicating that I had perilous psychological and moral problems causing me to seek refuge in a forgiving Church. In doing so, I had betrayed myself. To this day, my acquiescence then still disappoints me. It is a moment that I can only regret but can never deny. And I had accused the archbishop of being intellectually dishonest! I had just signed an untruthful document to make several church bureaucrats feel good and righteous. I was told that the laicization papers would be completed and approved by Rome six to nine months later.

As my fiancée and I began to make June 1970 plans to accommodate the ecclesiastical bureaucracy, we were rebuffed by her high school nun principal and by her local parish priest, a man whom I had actually recommended in writing be made pastor. When we requested to have our marriage at either place, we were told that only the archbishop could decide where and when we were to marry.

On November 11, 1969, I wrote a lengthy letter to Archbishop Dearden outlining my plans for marriage and my decision to remain in the community as a college professor. He waited until December 9, 1969, to respond. In his equally lengthy letter, he addressed the scandal that would exist if I did what I had planned. Up to this point, he and his canon lawyer priest in charge of the diocesan tribunal had selectively failed to inform me that our marriage could only take place *privately* at a place of their decision, with maybe a few guests at their choosing, with an officiating priest of their choosing. He outlined this officially in his scandal-drenched missive to me. All was done to humiliate the applicant into submission in the name of holiness and sparing scandal to the community as he perceived it. "What rubbish," as the British would say.

What I was told by a good source probably also would have happened: the archbishop would have insisted that I no longer live in the community where I was a priest due to the continued scandal; he probably would have insisted that I resign from the college there and find employment elsewhere. So I was told. I never gave the process the chance. This procedure also was confirmed as standard by Eugene Kennedy in the book he wrote in 2002 entitled *The Unhealed Wound*.

My last communications by letter to the archbishop reinforced discussions that I had had with him and my feeling of surprise that he would not allow two faithful families a chance to be one in a respectful way. I wrote the following simple letter to him on December 17, 1969:

> Archbishop Dearden,
> The position elaborated in your reply to my request is an unrealistic one. Your suggestion that our marriage must lack witnesses, save your choices, is unacceptable to Donna and me.
>
> To have each of our immediate and closest friends at our marriage celebration is presumed by any reasonable man; we would not even consider eliminating these people from our wedding. Your alternative is not really an alternative.
>
> Should we be unable to have our marriage celebrated in the Catholic Church with my brother as priest and at least our immediate families present, Donna and I shall find a truly Christian church willing to share the joy and happiness and love that is so much the style of our two families.

In return, the archbishop wrote back to me on December 26, 1969, the day before my twenty-eighth birthday, reiterating his concern of scandal in the broader community:

Marvin,

I am very disappointed that you chose not to address yourself to the central concern of my last letter to you (i.e. my words: the issue of scandal in the community). As bishop of Detroit, I must be concerned about the hurt that could come to the total community. Furthermore, as I tried to point out to you, the restrictions attached to the marriage ceremony of a priest are put there by the Holy Father, and I do not have it within my power to set these aside.

In point of fact, there is a prior issue that must be recognized. An indult that lifts the priestly obligation of celibacy is given only on the assurance that no scandal will be occasioned by it. The good of the whole local Church must be considered.

Because I have no wish to bring hurt to anyone, I would still welcome the opportunity to explain in person to both of your parents the very compelling reasons which moved me to write to you as I did in my last letter.

His first letter to me addressed me as "Father," and this last one as "Marvin." We never communicated with each other directly nor saw one another in person after those missives were exchanged.

Marriage

That March, nine months after I had resigned from the priesthood, Donna and I decided to marry one another at a small candlelit ceremony at the local Presbyterian church in a chapel reserved for non-members of the congregation. Forty of our closest family and friends celebrated with us. The Presbyterian pastor—Paul Markham—a true Christian gentleman officiated. My best man—Bernie Mullin—was a slightly older priest whom I had befriended in the same town during the two years in the ministry; he had been my salvation and mentor on many occasions and shared the same space on the needs of the Church. To the day of his death, he never indicated the problem that he may have had with the chancery or the archbishop when it was discovered that he was best man for a renegade clergyman in the town where he was still functioning as priest. Today, I still hold him in my heart as my best man, courageous and true to the end on living a principled life.

Donna began a beautiful tradition that evening by being married in her mother's wedding gown, wearing a gold cross that her mother, her Mimi Reau, and her

Grand-Mimi Valequette all had worn at their weddings. When our daughter Támara was married, she was the third generation to wear the same dress. Since 1941 and every twenty-eight-plus years after, a Reau, a Rimer, and a Josaitis have walked down the aisle in the same simple, white satin dress—unfaded over the decades—merely slightly adapted to meet stylistic differences. Mom Rimer lived to see her granddaughter replicate the memories of 1941 and 1970 in 1998.

Three hundred guests partied at the local hotel that evening in the same town where I was functioning anew as a full-time college professor. In finding the love that God ordained for his creation, a man and a woman found themselves in God's hands, apart from the Catholic Church's blessing. How ironic! We never formally left the Church, but—in fact—we left the Catholic Church peacefully in our own style as we left the steps of a Presbyterian chapel that March twenty-fifth evening in 1970. We continued to live and work in the community for another six years before beginning the new mobile corporate and international phase of our life together. It was here that we began our family and nurtured our two young daughters and infant son.

Dad and Mom Rimer were second parents for me. Donna felt the same about my parents, who loved her as the daughter that they always wanted to have. Her father was a gentle and quiet man who had similar qualities to my father. He generally had a pipe in his hand and enjoyed spending time conversing, playing cards with us, or helping us by sharing his talented handyman and carpentry skills.

Mom was a practical and honest person who also loved our company. Her home was our home. Her time was our time. Her mothering skills became loving grandmothering skills when we presented her with her first grandchildren to love. It was wonderful to have new parents who accepted me as their older son.

While Dad Rimer was an only child, his stepbrother, Owen Scott, along with his wife, Eunice, in nearby Ohio welcomed me as a new nephew. Mom's family had lived in Monroe for two centuries. Her mother Cecilia Reau, Donna's Mimi, who still lived only a block away, became my new Mimi. It was wonderful for me to have a Mimi again after more than two decades without. I now also had many new uncles, aunts, and cousins. The Reau and LaPrad families accepted me into their families, remarkable especially since I had months before been functioning as a priest in their community—and a rather conservative community at that! Mom and Mimi, I am told, were frequently asked what it was like having a former priest in the family. They would just shrug and say simply that it was like having another wonderful son or grandson to love.

Donna was accepted without question by all of my uncles, aunts, and cousins from the Girards—most of whom lived in southern Michigan. They, like Donna's family, were pleased to welcome the baby of the family's bride into the family. We were included in all family events. Consequently, our children became part of the heritages long evident throughout both of our family traditions.

While our first home was an apartment twenty-five minutes north of town, we eventually moved into Monroe after our first year of marriage and established ourselves a block away from Mom and Dad Rimer, and Mimi Reau. Until we were able to purchase our first home when it became vacant across the street, Mom and Dad were our landlords. What a wonderful environment to raise our three babies during our first six years together. We were rooted in a community where nearly all of Donna's family lived. And we lived just south of most of my parents' families. So our young family lived and experienced a four-generational reality during their formative years. For our young children, their Papa Gerald, Mimi Ada, and their one Grand-Mimi lived just a block away, with Papa Frank and Mimi Margaret less than an hour by car. My father had retired when his first grandchild was born so that he and my mother would have plenty of time to spend with grandchildren … and spend time they did! Our children relished every second spent with all their involved grandparents.

Mom and Dad Rimer had married in Monroe, Michigan, three months and a week before I was born. Like my parents, death ended a beautiful and long marriage fifteen months prior to their fiftieth anniversary. As a consequence, our children have come from several generations of long marriages. In truth, we don't know of any divorce in either of our direct lineages.

We were so fortunate to have both sets of our parents' constant love and support in our own marriage. We were fortunate to have them as dear friends as well as nouveau parents. What memories these four parent treasures gave to our children who distinguished each by adding the given name of each to Mimi or Papa.

Our last contact with the archbishop was through his chancellor, another canon lawyer monsignor who telephoned me in early June 1970, gloatingly informing me that the laicization papers had been sent from Rome to Detroit—"You and Donna can now be married in the Church and leave behind your life of sin." The telephone conversation was sharply quick and to the point. I told the monsignor to do whatever he wanted to do with the papers—they meant nothing to us. And I closed by telling him to inform the archbishop that "the two of you may find some perverse joy in claiming that we are not married and are living in sin. As far as my bride and I are concerned, we are married in our own hearts, in the eyes of God, and in the hearts of a community more Christian in spirit than either of you ever can experience in canon law." That was the last official encounter that I had with an official representative of the Church that had ordained me a "priest forever, according to the order of Melchisedech."

Burying the
Last Remnant

I had made so many changes and adaptations throughout my life. However, it is true that you can take the boy out of the seminary but not the seminary out of the boy. I struggled for many years with the idea of the "indelible mark": the belief that once a priest, the individual is permanently marked as a priest. It was the last mindset that kept me from total freedom. It never was a conscious problem, but it would bubble forth from my unconscious periodically, even in nightly dreams for many decades. Often I would feel that I was marked as different, special in the eyes of God beyond other men. I would even conjecture that there was a special overlay or protection in life due to an event that happened at the cathedral that June morning in 1967. It took me a very long time to alter my psyche to the reality that this was a superimposed paradigm from a belief system meant to control and authenticate a particular authoritative mindset.

For over twenty-five years, I continued to reflect on the "indelible mark" theologically imbedded into my psyche when I was ordained "forever according to the order of Melchisedech." Amazing how powerful an implantation can be when one has prepared twelve years for that moment. Now and then, I would even dream at night about various events that had occurred during the seminary years or my two years as a parish priest. During my conscious hours at times, I would reflect on the "mark" and felt that maybe I even had a continuing relationship with the Divine, not accorded most men: I was special. I was almost haunted by the idea that God's finger still moved and directed me in predetermined directions for an end and a purpose unknown to me.

I didn't bury this last vestige of the priesthood until the 1990s during a vacation that my spouse, Donna, and I took to Colorado. We were visiting friends just outside of Colorado Springs, two former priest friends and their spouses, who as it happened had both been former nuns. The six of us had varying shades of awareness and interest in Native American spirituality. One of my friends had discovered years earlier a relatively new tradition among the Lakota Sioux entitled the "circle of friends," complete with stimulus prayer cards and an accompanying text of meditative readings. Since we had not been together for a while, we decided that it would be fitting to gather one evening as we had in the past around a candle-lit table as a circle of friends invoking the presence of our ancestors through the Great Spirit in us all. Present with us, however, was a stranger to Donna and me—a quiet man who lived across the street, a neighbor joining the six of us for the evening in the "circle."

The process is relatively easy and unencumbered. After Great Spirit is addressed and invoked, each person in turn selects at random a prayer card. The prayer card has an inspirational theme and directs its present "holder" to read to the group a particular passage from the published text. The reader then reflects momentarily and shares with those present how these words of wisdom have particular meaning in his or her life. Anyone can then comment and brief discussion ensues before the next person in the circle continues the process until the last has had a turn. Having participated many times in this ceremony, I can attest to its beauty and power. I have yet to walk away without profound new insights into my life and have always been strengthened meaningfully by the process. This night was no different; in fact, it was monumental in my personal growth and development. And the inspiring moment came from an observation from the stranger, the one person in the "circle of friends" whom I had never met before and have never seen since, implanted perhaps from Great Spirit as a passerby who was instrumental in freeing my spirit.

The man whom I didn't know looked up over the rim of his bifocals and said, "I am not a Catholic, but it seems to me that you are allowing a mere idea, believed by some but unable to be proved by any, to prevent you from being totally human. Hey, man, you are just like all of us and there isn't anything wrong with that. Get on with your wonderful life, guy, and be thankful for every blessing that is yours."

I was speechless.

I buried this "Superman" mental construct and former belief in the 1990s, finally—for once and for all. No more dreams. No more gnawing paradigms from a former existence.

Our Love Story

Donna and I celebrated our fortieth anniversary in 2010. For us, *It's a Wonderful Life* is not the name of a fictional movie only; it describes our life together. We have lived and continue to live a wonderful life together. Our three loving children, their terrific spouses, and six beautiful grandchildren are exactly what any couple could happily envision. Our children and grandchildren continue to "melt" us. They are the living attestations of our love. Happiness today could only be more complete if our four parents, who themselves had meaningful and long marriages, were still walking amidst us, experiencing our joys through the eyes of the generation that made this all possible. At our anniversary celebration, our children—who throughout the years have always managed to select a beautifully appropriate Hallmark card—gifted us with this one:

> The story of our family
> is made up of many things—
> from silly jokes
> to good-night kisses,

from nicknames
to summer vacations,
from hard good-byes
to the most joyous homecomings.
The story of our family
is made up of love
and time
and memory…
all the things that really matter.
And at the heart of our story
will always be
the two of you.

Donna and I raised our two daughters and one son in the USA, Canada, the United Kingdom, and have moved sixteen times with memories to last many lifetimes. Looking back at our individual lives and our life together, we realize how unbelievably blessed and fortunate we have been. Parents, grandparents, children, grandchildren, relatives, friends, and teachers have all contributed to the charmed lives we live. Truly, we were raised by a village of caring people, the most important of which have been duly highlighted. Put simply, our love story is an involved, complex, happy narrative that has happy endings.

But most important, our marriage has been liberated from obligation, guilt, and Roman canon law. Ours has been liberation from organized church to a spiritual journey, which is the true core of all religious beliefs. Our children were raised to be totally responsible for their actions without mediation from anyone else outside of themselves, to be tolerant of cultural and religious differences, and with no means of excusing inappropriate behavior through any type of religious scapegoat machinations. Too often, people raised with the imposition of strong religious thought excuse their own actions and write them off as simply forgivable, and then they continue to replicate the same behavior over and over again, taking no personal ownership or responsibility.

We decided to raise our children without an organized church but with deep family and spiritual values. Today, all of our children have spirituality but not necessarily an organized religious expression: one of them is an active Episcopalian, one is un-churched, and one of them has adapted to a cultural Hindu spirituality out of deep respect and love for his Indian-born spouse. All of them have made their own choices and totally accept the challenges and responsibilities for their decisions. In kind, our six grandchildren are being raised with different spiritual influences. Throughout our four decades together, we have deepened our spiritual awareness by minimizing our contact with the prescriptively religious.

The Church's Challenge

My reason for telling this story is the backdrop that it provides for the current behavior of some Catholic clergy and clergy from other organized religious churches. Pedophiliac and sexually aberrant behavior may be rooted in the same sources. I am saddened by its enormity and the resulting attempt to absolve church and hierarchy or teachings from any cause-effect responsibility. The truth is that most priests and clergymen are fine and upright persons. An equal truth, I propose, is that church teaching on sexuality may indeed foster the problem in the Catholic Church and may create, in a very complicated way, the aberrant clergyman.

This is what I now continue to see. The dogmatic positions taken on human sexuality and other key issues by the Catholic Church need drastic change. Pope John Paul II and the current Pope Benedict XVI continue successively to reverse the more liberating theologies, which emerged during the 1960s as spearheaded by Pope John XXIII during the Second Vatican Council. Soon this distant memory of a Church beginning to be revitalized and re-inspirited with an earlier Christian élan sadly and tragically may become merely an historical footnote. Pope Benedict XVI's return to an even more rigid neo-conservatism within the Catholic Church perhaps might lead to a smaller reality that resembles more the Medieval Church that emerged and flourished for so many centuries.

Regarding the current reiteration of its traditional and unbending positions on sexuality, the Vatican's views today may be rooted in an ancient order and then coated with medieval mistrust of human sexuality combined with a strange connection to the world of evil.

I question the basic mistrust of women espoused in so many ways and later codified into dogmas. It begins with Eve viewed by the ancients as the first woman, in one scriptural account created second from a part of man, the male obviously being God's first choice. She is second to man and becomes the temptress of an innocent Adam and, consequently, surely a person one can never trust completely. The role of woman is still taught as submissive to man in marriage. Literature abounds with this concept of the deceptive, naughty woman. By the thirteenth century, the scholastics, headed by none other than St. Thomas Aquinas, referred to woman as an inferior man, undeveloped, missing an essential organ.

But never fret. Mary arrived as the perfect woman who was not conceived as other women; nor did she have sex like most married women. Rather, she is proclaimed a perpetual physical virgin in marriage and was impregnated by God directly. (Biblical scholars have pointed out that the scriptural word for young maiden is the same as that used for virgin.) As the new Eve, Mary could not have been tainted by the flesh with its needs to fulfill sex drives. Nor could she carry the God-man Jesus who, in deciding to become human, could not have been carried in a normal human womb. He could not be a part of a normal woman's total nature and its cycles, viewed as dirty and impure. So God becomes man, but not through a typical birth or life after birth in a marriage of a normal set of parents. Instead, the Church gives us the *asexual* God-Son living with a virgin mother and celibate protector, who is only an apparent husband and father! Is this truly God's version or man's perversion of the God becoming man story?

Furthermore, celibacy then becomes enshrined somewhere before the dark ages of Europe as sanctifying. Issues like masturbation are viewed as sinful, justified by a misinterpretation of only one text in the Old Testament referring to Onan's spilling of his seed rather than agreeing to have sex, as custom provided, with his dead brother's wife. Having sex for pro-creativity emerges and is taught as the only justification for this otherwise unsanctified and banal or "worldly" human practice. Catholic theology and teachings then reinforced this medieval view of a human kind, which fled from the garden of Eden ashamed of its wrongdoings and aware of its sexuality, which was dirty and ungodly. Is it any wonder that celibacy became exalted and legally legitimized as required for those who would give themselves to God totally? A man and a woman having sex can't be viewed as giving themselves totally to God because of their connection to evil and sinful behavior.

Is it any wonder that the Church canonizes mostly male, celibate, clerical, and papal individuals who have been given this "gift of God," celibacy? More of a gift than the beauty, wonder, and power of sex. Rarely are married persons canonized as saints unless they are widowed and, therefore, *asexual.* A few nods have been given to martyrs, regardless of sex, and a few nuns and virgins have been elevated to the club of sainthood. As well, a few royal or wealthy patrons of the Church have made the cut. Consistently, the celibate Vatican has given its faithful mirror images of themselves as examples of truly virtuous life, intimating that anything sexual is second best in the eyes of God.

Even today in the twenty-first century, the Vatican continues to proclaim beatification and sainthood for dominantly priests, popes, and nuns—celibates. Note the current excitement in Rome on the beatification of Pope John Paul II, who fits the pattern.

So many Catholic teachings are corollaries in disguise of this medieval and distorted view of human sexuality and of the inferior nature of woman. There remains still a prohibition on ordaining married men as priests or permitting single priests to marry despite an unbelievable need throughout the Catholic communities of the world. Better to self-destruct and live with an ever-aging group of male priests than to defile this "calling from God." Only as a political accommodation to entice certain clerical converts have exceptions been made. Hence, the occasional married Anglican or Orthodox married priests who were accepted into the Catholic Church. And this usually is hushed and not advertised.

But at least the early Christian Church had married men who were priests. God forbid that a woman could ever become a priest; after all, God chose to become a man (male) and not a woman. Despite conflicting beliefs that in Christ there is no male or female, the undercurrent of Eve persists where ordination is concerned. Traditionalists even within the Anglican communities continue to eschew their relatively recent decision to ordain some women. The Catholic Church proudly stands as the protector of a more ancient order, faithful to a male-dominated theology surrounding the creation story. As recently as the summer of 2010, the Catholic Church proclaimed that ordaining women as priests is part of a list of the most serious of sins, which include pedophilia, heresy, schism, and apostasy. As chairman of the United States Conference of Catholic Bishops, Archbishop Donald Wuerl of Washington even asserted: "The Catholic Church, through its long and constant teaching, holds that ordination has been, from the beginning, reserved to men, a fact which cannot be changed despite changing times."[3] Another incredible testimonial to the criticism leveled against the ecclesiastical hierarchy that they are indeed a "boy's club"!

Without belaboring the point, the Catholic Church also continues to deny the role of artificial birth control measures. Birth control beyond abstinence is not viewed as a woman's right but rather as a prescription to continue her defiled state with the effect of fostering an irresponsible world population growth. And abortion, even under the ignominy and tragedy of rape, is not justified. In effect, this continues the authoritative role of a powerful Vatican and its emissaries because of its political implications. To be sure, this position also continues to reinforce the pre-eminence of the male over the female rooted in the interpretation of the garden of Eden.

Yet another sexual issue at its core is the Church's official position on divorce. Sanctioned divorce and remarriage are still only permitted if the husband and wife live as brother and sister, or if some canon law exception can be found. In my brief tenure as a priest, I became aware that the Vatican was able to be maneuvered in its interpretation of canon law exceptions if the right stipend was able to arrive at the opportune time on the appropriate cleric's desk in Rome. Little wonder that some strange exceptions to divorce and remarriage periodically become public and notorious in the case of influential and wealthy patrons of the Vatican, justified because some little known canon law had been violated, justifying an annulment of a previous marriage. In some of these cases, even a second splashy church wedding is permitted.

I also ponder about other avoidances that the hierarchy will leave for historians and archivists to figure out. Isn't it a strange anomaly that men were castrated in order to have angelic, rather than masculine, voices in the papal choir? The last of these "castrati" died little more than fifty years ago. That this practice was justified and sanctioned at the highest level of the Church is quite revealing in itself. And today, I know of no concerted effort on the part of the hierarchy either to de-link the implication in the minds of many that pedophilia is simply an advanced stage or progression of homosexuality. Better to remain silent about such unnatural conditions. An issue like this is not "cause célèbre" for a neo-conservative hierarchy more prone to hope that silence on such matters rather than proactive and educational involvement will cause embarrassments like these eventually to just go away.

Catholic boys and girls are presented over and over again in catechetical repetition how God abhors and punishes the sins of the flesh. They are given heroes and heroines who are sexless creatures and are taught that these people were holy in the eyes of God. To defile one's body can mean permanent punishment by an unforgiving God. Hence, there are Marian devotions to the "model of purity," one who will intercede for the unworthy sexually weak. Is it any wonder that growing up in this environment may encourage the truly sexually hung-up boys to seek salvation by joining a celibate clergy?

And the bishops, pope, and all clergy in the main continue to reinforce these paradigms of holiness, virtue, and stifled human behavior—almost a self-fulfilling justification.

If the saints of God continually reinforced are sexless, then what happens to the human drives and natural inclinations that are inappropriately and immaturely handled? Unfortunately, the powerful position that the clergyman has often can tip those individuals who have consumed these medieval paradigms and digested them without balance to become imbalanced themselves in the process. This reality is not a late twentieth century or early twenty-first century clerical problem. This clerical sexual aberration has existed for centuries, covered up by the well-intentioned as well as the ill-intentioned. The discovery and media coverage is what is new. Fortunately, a more educated, less docile laity may be emerging to challenge the clandestine behavior and teachings of the Catholic Church. But, maybe not, if neo-conservatism has its way.

The Need to Change

The current pope and bishops continue to "rule" as princes of the church rather than as servants. This paradigm needs total overhauling: cardinal ermine clothing, episcopal palaces, and all. All of these trappings of a past age are further exacerbated by the strange concept of "papal infallibility," an authoritative Catholic construct that, in my opinion, no longer has viability. Papal infallibility is the belief that the pope is free from error in teaching the universal church on matters of faith or morals. Rationally and logically examining those proclamations and doctrines as defined over the last 150 years—especially the dogmas about Mary—should be sufficient to closet this concept once and for all. The last two Marian dogmas, the Immaculate Conception and the Assumption of Mary, body and soul after death into heaven in particular, are theological stretches with questionable justification. These dogmas continue to be a major divisive feature in ecumenical dialogue within the broader Christian world.

Believing that the Catholic Church or Christianity is the one true belief system created by God will continue to produce and foster arrogant and prejudicially narrow masses of people. Canon law is used to regulate this belief system and reinforces guilt. A changing paradigm should emerge that realizes that all the great religions and religious movements have, beneath their periphery, cores of truth and insights in the spirit world. None is exclusive. When we can seek spiritual truth without re-interpreting through our own paradigms, we will emerge the wiser … perhaps even the more God-like.

Continuing to foster the Western view of man as "apart from" rather than a "part of" nature will ultimately destroy us all. This is not a political bowing to Al Gore or anyone else. What is true for the physical universe also applies to mankind. Man and woman as well as their bodies' offspring are a part of nature. The Church too often, as I have indicated above, is unwilling to view this reality as a simple truth. Instead, the dark overlay or interpretation of evil enters into the equation. The fall of man, as interpreted by the Church as the original sin of our parents passed on to all of mankind requiring redemption, places man outside of this nature. Actually, the Church is uncomfortable with the concept that human nature is good. The element of evil justifies so much of the Church's power and authority over its believers. Somehow, if we can begin to act as though the God in all living things exists, we will be transformed and so will our world.

Changing these paradigmatic ways of viewing religion, especially within the context of Catholicism, is what is truly needed today. If the Church only castigates the few (but far too many) priests being under-covered as "ill," and scapegoats the real problems, nothing will change.

The changes in sexual paradigms will permit women as equal partners in life and faith, both as clergypersons and laity. A clergy based on character and not sexuality is required to move forward. The changes in authority paradigms will permit the hierarchy and papacy to reposition themselves as spiritual servants and leaders, not guardians of control, protocol, law, and defenders of a past order. A new and fresh exploration of nature and man's part in it, moving away from conquering and misusing, will free the universe.

Transcending Religious Bureaucracy

All of these issues will help to de-reify (a sociological term, which means making something alive into a thing—changing spirit into lifelessness) a Church and a clergy that have cloaked reality with the mystical and the legal/prescriptive. In effect, over centuries they have turned an original spirit-driven reality into a bureaucracy that protects its place and controls its people. Faith is really destroyed in a reified organization (called Church) where obedience to law becomes paramount.

The same process happens in the business world. A visionary develops small businesses and creates a fresh environment for people to work as a close-knit family. Few regulations exist initially. People talk out their needs. Following this, the business grows and people are hired to write the rules and regulations. Then, the business gets even bigger and organizational structures are put in place. Western corporate organizational charts are similar to those of the Catholic Church who copied theirs from the

Imperial Rome of Caesar. So reification occurs through-out life as men organize. And then, people are recruited to "recreate" the freshness that originally was intended and breathe new life into the organization. Attempts are made in man's organizations to try and "de-reify" to make them en-spirited again.

In my opinion, as it is now from an outsider looking into where he once was, the Catholic Church and Christianity as we know them must die and be reborn with a new, far-reaching spiritual message. Such is the nature of any great institution. Unless it changes, it may become a museum piece. The great wisdom of the ages through other "prophetic" insights, be they Druid, Muslim, Buddhist, Hindu, Confucian, Taoist, Mormon, Roman Catholic, Orthodox Christian, Pentecostal, Quaker, Protestant, Judaic, or whatever organized religious belief system, needs to be turned free, amalgamated, en-spirited, de-institutionalized, and de-bureaucratized. A new order of tolerant believers whose humanity is enriched and broadened, not shackled and imprisoned, by an élan, a spiritual force that transcends the organizational. For example, Martin Luther's spirit was eventually reified and bureaucratized; hence, the spirit stopped growing, stopped questioning and searching. So it was with all the reformers and off-shoot branches of Christianity. Once growth and learning stop, the spirit dies and legal prescription with its rules takes over. It is the Taliban mentality found in every major religious organization today.

When Talmudic law, canon law, defined Doctrines of Catechism take over, it is time for a cleaning of the house.

Until this happens, all churches and religious groups will be entrapped in their own closets and various types of guilt with inaccurate worldviews will pervade and compete. They may even war against each other as their institutions become part and parcel of the nation, economy, and cultural way of life they now espouse. Man, in turn, will be crying for freedom. The aberrant clergyman or religious leader is really a voice of entrapped guilt crying for this freedom from past imprisoning paradigms.

We all can learn much from the Native American spirituality, which, in all its simplicity and sometimes inaccurate scientific worldview, has not tended to be reified and codified as other spiritual systems. Hinduism has some of the same non-dogmatic simplicity. Western European man, carrying the cross with the sword, felt justified in trying to root out this spirituality in the name of God and truth, as they defined these realities. The Church softened the natives, replacing their ancient paradigms with new ones to make way for the conquistador. European cultural imperialists acted in the name of God to torture "pagans" and convert "heathens" to the truth as they defined and believed it. Fortunately, the campaign has not totally succeeded in wiping out the Native American traditions or the traditions and simple belief systems of so many cultures throughout the world.

A Dysfunctional Church: Pedophilia

It is my hope that others will give voice—whether from a psychological, philosophical, historical, sociological, theological, "any logical" point of view—using the current springboard of aberrant sexual behavior as well as cultural strife as springboards for new birth. If educated people remain silent, others living in the closed prison of a Church we once thought wonderful will not have the courage to recreate. The Church spreads so much fear and guilt, making people dependent on the authority they believe God has placed in this institution. We have a wonderful opportunity to publish to a world—at least on this side of the Atlantic and Pacific—that may be ready to hear and digest a new way of thinking about the role of the Church in people's lives. The time is ripe. People in all cultures and religious traditions are concerned about the world's order. Now, these people of good will need to address religious thought as presently institutionalized.

There are many former and active clergy or religious who have analyzed the religious dysfunction and brokenness existing in belief systems today. There are those who will work only to root out and destroy the sexually aberrant priests, thinking that this will solve the problem at hand and restore the Church to its former glory. I, for one, who was in the organized Church and was one of its clergy, look from the outside in now and hope that more people will realize that the cover-up may continue by a hierarchy bent on keeping its power and control in place, a hierarchy not looking where they should be looking, i.e. at themselves.

A few years ago Bernard Law, then Boston's cardinal, indicated that if God wanted him to continue serving God and his people, he would, and that people should realize that he never intended anyone to get hurt. This followed the priest sex scandal where the Cardinal had reassigned a known priest pedophiliac rather than face the horrible reality existing in his diocese and elsewhere squarely and head-on. Cardinal Law was speaking like most bishops in his situation. He, and they, really didn't get the message. Commentaries from equally naïve priests are periodically published suggesting that the Church will recover from this sex scandal as it has from other scandals and all of us will be able to get back to the way things were. I call this the "living in Oz" syndrome. These religious commentators don't get it either.

Over the past decade, the clergy and the pope have continued to indicate that it is better to hide one's head in the sand. We even hear occasional references from the Vatican to the distinctly "American" or "Irish" problem, which doesn't really exist in other places in the world, especially not among Italian clerics. And the current pope even protects his beloved "Fatherland." They don't seem to get it either.

Pope Benedict XVI continues to play "cat and mouse" on the issues of reassigning pedophiliac priests during his diocesan experiences as a bishop. It is unfortunate that the spirit of a brilliant forty-two-year-old theologian, a young Josef Ratzinger (the future Benedict XVI), didn't endure. As I was resigning from the priesthood in 1969 for the reasons that I have shared, he was imagining a Church simplified and de-reified, closer to its simple gospel first century reality. From a German radio station, he prophesied:

> From today's crisis, a church will emerge tomorrow that will have lost a great deal. She will be small and, to a large extent, will have to start from the beginning. She will no longer be able to fill many of the buildings created in her period of great splendor. Because of the smaller number of her followers, she will lose many of her privileges in society. Contrary to what has happened until now, she will present herself much more as a community of volunteers … As a small community, she will demand much more from the initiative of each of her members, and she will certainly also acknowledge new forms of ministry and will raise up to the priesthood proven Christians who have other jobs … It will make her poor and a church of the little people … All this will require time. The process will be slow and painful.[4]

Unfortunately, Josef Ratzinger went to Rome in 1981 and spent two decades being groomed as a cardinal in the traditional imperial Roman papacy that continues to create a faith crisis for those who would want to see divine genuine simplicity rather than continued pomposity. In short, as a victim to the powerful Catholic Roman Curia, he lost his ideals. In the process, he gained enough internal political power to become pope. What a price to pay! More seriously, any hope for change in the Catholic Church for the immediate future has also been lost.

The spirit of the second Vatican Council, which charged me and influenced me as a theological student and as a young priest, is becoming a distant memory amidst yet another neo-conservative papacy wanting to return to a former age of glory and of power.

For whatever it is worth, I am no longer silent; my grand silence is broken after having taken many roads to get to where I am today.

Conclusions

To conclude, I propose that the Catholic Church, in particular, and a variety of Christian offspring support an unhealthy, irrational, destructive belief system backed by policies, practices, and organizational structures that often are intellectually dishonest, lacking in integrity, and medieval in their worldview of reality. Many of us realized that in one way or another and decided to change the direction of our lives. The intellectual dishonesty in the Church and its clergy and hierarchy, along with a belief system that I could no longer represent, led me to turn directions at age twenty-seven, after spending twelve of those years studying to achieve priesthood. And so I have had forty-plus years of relative silence.

A short stint with Episcopalians, twice as a vestryman, represented almost four years. During that period and now observing the painful anguish currently tearing apart worldwide Anglicanism, I have concluded that organized religious groups have the same inherent problem that human organizations all have: "sticking to the knitting," keeping the original spirit alive, avoiding the prescriptive and judgmental. The rest of my life has been un-churched, but a spiritual existence and growth continues to take place nonetheless.

I have been fortunate to have a spouse that has journeyed in the same direction as I. We believe that the Church is not in crisis today only; it *has been* in crisis for decades and centuries. The sexual behavior of its priests is only an external reflection of the systemic reality that reinforces and created that reality. Fortunately, "God writes straight with crooked lines," as the Portuguese proverb proclaims. I believe that the apparent assaults to organized religious groups and disaffection with many of their teachings happening in the world is a positive opportunity for people of all belief systems to grow and develop in new directions, freeing themselves from the old paradigms of the holy and the sacred.

Epilogue

"The Road Not Taken"
Robert Frost, 1915

Two roads diverged in a yellow wood,
And sorry I could not travel both
And be a traveler, long I stood
And looked down one as far as I could
To where it bent in the undergrowth;

Then took the other, as just as fair,
And having perhaps the better claim,
Because it was grassy and wanted wear;
Though as for that the passing there
Had worn them really about the same.

And both that morning equally lay
In leaves no step had trodden black.
Oh, I kept the first for another day!
Yet knowing how way leads on to way,
I doubted if I should ever come back.

I shall be telling this with a sigh
Somewhere ages and ages hence:
Two roads diverged in a wood, and I—
I took the one less traveled by,
And that has made all the difference.

And that has made all the difference.

Endnotes

1   Joyce Carol Oates, *We Were The Mulvaneys,* Penguin, N.Y., N.Y., 1996, p.230.

2   A reference to the revered Old Testament King and Priest of Salem who offered bread and wine to Abraham in the Book of Genesis. Catholic tradition tied this type of sacrificial offering as applicable to the priesthood of Jesus in St. Paul's Epistle to the Hebrews. The Catholic Church emphasized the "forever" nature of priesthood, especially throughout the ordination rite as an "indelible" mark given by God to the newly ordained priest.

3   As reported in the *NY Times,* "Vatican Revises Abuse Process, but Causes Stir," by Rachel Donadio, July 15, 2010.

4   As reported in *Time Magazine,* "The Trial of Benedict XVI," by Jeff Israely and Howard Chua-Egan, June 7, 2010, p.43.